www.osha.gov

Employers are responsible for providing a safe and healthful workplace for their employees. OSHA's role is to assure the safety and health of America's working men and women by setting and enforcing standards; providing training, outreach and education; establishing partnerships; and encouraging continual improvement in workplace safety and health.

This informational booklet provides a general overview of a particular topic related to OSHA standards. It does not alter or determine compliance responsibilities in OSHA standards or the *Occupational Safety and Health Act of 1970*. Because interpretations and enforcement policy may change over time, you should consult current OSHA administrative interpretations and decisions by the Occupational Safety and Health Review Commission and the courts for additional guidance on OSHA compliance requirements.

This information is available to sensory impaired individuals upon request. Voice phone: (202) 693-1999; teletypewriter (TTY) number: (877) 889-5627.

Edwin G. Foulke, Jr.
Assistant Secretary of Labor for
Occupational Safety and Health

Hospitals and Community Emergency Response

What You Need to Know

U.S. Department of Labor

Occupational Safety and Health Administration

OSHA 3152-3R
2008

Contents

This guidance document is not a standard or regulation, and it creates no new legal obligations. The document is advisory in nature, informational in content, and is intended to assist employers in providing a safe and healthful workplace. *The Occupational Safety and Health Act* requires employers to comply with hazard-specific safety and health standards promulgated by OSHA or by a State with an OSHA-approved State Plan. In addition, pursuant to Section 5(a)(1), the General Duty Clause of the Act, employers must provide their employees with a workplace free from recognized hazards likely to cause death or serious physical harm. Employers can be cited for violating the General Duty Clause if there is a recognized hazard and they do not take reasonable steps to prevent or abate the hazard. However, failure to implement these recommendations is not, in itself, a violation of the General Duty Clause. Citations can only be based on standards, regulations, and the General Duty Clause.

ACRONYMS

CFR	Code of Federal Regulations
DHS	U.S. Department of Homeland Security
DOT	U.S. Department of Transportation
EMS	Emergency Medical Service
EMT	Emergency Medical Technician
EPA	Environmental Protection Agency
EPCRA	Emergency Planning and Community Right-to-Know Act
ERP	Emergency Response Plan
HAZMAT	Hazardous Materials
HAZWOPER	Hazardous Waste Operations and Emergency Response
ICS	Incident Command System
JCAHO	Joint Commission on Accreditation of Healthcare Organizations
LEPC	Local Emergency Planning Committee
MSDSs	Material Safety Data Sheets
NCP	National Contingency Plan
NIMS	National Incident Management System
NRF	National Response Framework (formerly National Response Plan)
OSHA	Occupational Safety and Health Administration
PPE	Personal Protective Equipment
SARA	Superfund Amendments and Reauthorization Act of 1986
SERC	State Emergency Response Commission
SHARP	Safety and Health Achievement Recognition Program
VPP	Voluntary Protection Programs

4

Introduction

Protecting healthcare workers who respond to emergencies involving hazardous substances is critical. Healthcare workers responding to emergencies may be exposed to chemical, biological, physical, or radioactive hazards. Hospitals providing emergency response services must be prepared to carry out their missions without jeopardizing the safety and health of their own and other employees. Of special concern are the situations where contaminated patients arrive at the hospital for triage (sorting) or definitive treatment following a major incident.

In many localities, the hospital has not been firmly integrated into the community emergency response system and may not be prepared to safely treat multiple casualties resulting from an incident involving hazardous substances. Increasing awareness of the need to protect healthcare workers and understanding the principal considerations in emergency response planning will help reduce the risk of employee exposure to hazardous substances.

(Note: This publication focuses on emergencies originating outside the hospital and does not address responses to internal hazardous material (HAZMAT) releases, e.g., release of ethylene oxide).

Background

Both the Occupational Safety and Health Administration (OSHA) and the Environmental Protection Agency (EPA) have regulations to protect employees dealing with hazardous waste operations and emergency response. Title III of the *Superfund Amendments and Reauthorization Act of 1986* (SARA) requires each state to establish a State Emergency Response Commission (SERC) that designates and coordinates the activities of Local Emergency Planning Committees (LEPCs). Under the National Response Framework (NRF)*, the LEPCs must develop a community emergency response plan (contingency plan) that contains emergency response methods and procedures to be followed by facility owners, police, hospitals, local emergency responders, and emergency medical personnel.

In planning for emergencies, LEPCs must designate a local hospital that has agreed to accept and treat victims of emergency incidents. The designated local hospital, which should have a representative participating in the LEPC or SERC, becomes part of the community emergency response organization.

SARA also directed that OSHA establish a comprehensive rule to protect employee health and safety during hazardous waste operations, including emergency responses to the release of hazardous substances. Accordingly, OSHA published the Hazardous Waste Operations and Emergency Response (HAZWOPER) standard, Title 29, Code of Federal Regulations (CFR) 1910.120 and 1926.65 (construction), which became effective in 1990. The 26 OSHA-approved State Plans have adopted HAZWOPER standards which are "at least as effective as" the federal OSHA standard and extend coverage to state and local government employers and employees. In states without OSHA-approved State Plans, state and local government employers and employees are covered by the EPA (40 CFR Part 311) with regard to the HAZWOPER standard.

* Effective March 22, 2008

The National Incident Management System (NIMS) and the National Response Framework (NRF)

The National Contingency Plan (NCP), which was revised under SARA to require communities to prepare local Emergency Response Plans (ERP), has been annexed to the National Response Framework (NRF). The NRF uses the framework of the National Incident Management System (NIMS) to provide the structure and mechanisms for the coordination of federal support during "an incident requiring a Coordinated Federal Response." The NRF, successor to the National Response Plan (NRP), focuses on effective response and short-term recovery. It also articulates the doctrine, principles and architecture by which the U.S. prepares for and responds to all-hazard disasters across all levels of government and all sectors and components of communities. The Department of Homeland Security (DHS) developed the NRF to inform emergency management practitioners by explaining the operating structures and resources routinely used by first responders and emergency managers at all levels of government. Compliance with the Incident Command System (ICS)[1], as provided by the NIMS and incorporated into the NRF, is consistent with using an incident command system under HAZWOPER. It describes how communities, states, the federal government and private-sector and nongovernmental partners apply these principles for a congruent, effective national response. In addition, it illustrates special circumstances where the federal government exercises a substantial role, including incidents where federal concerns are involved and catastrophic incidents where a state would require significant support. It sets the foundation for first responders, decision-makers and supporting components to provide an integrated national response. (Note: The NRF is available on the Department of Homeland Security's website at www.dhs.gov; ICS training information is available on the Federal Emergency Management Agency's website at www.fema.gov.)

[1]Incident Command System is an organized approach to effectively control and manage operations at an emergency incident.

Emergency Response Plans

OSHA's HAZWOPER standard requires employers, including hospitals, to plan for emergencies if they expect to assign their employees to respond to emergencies involving hazardous substances. A hospital designated by a LEPC or hazardous waste site as a decontamination facility must have an ERP which addresses, among other things, decontamination, personal protective equipment (PPE), and the roles and functions of trained personnel.

OSHA also recommends the development of an ERP for any other hospitals that may receive and treat victims whose treatment may present decontamination issues, even if they have not been designated as decontamination facilities. In an emergency, victims may self refer to the nearest hospital, even if it is not the one designated for decontamination.

The emergency response section of HAZWOPER (29 CFR 1910.120(q)) outlines required ERP elements. A hospital may use the local community emergency response plan or the state emergency response plan, or both, as part of its emergency response plan. The hospital does not have to duplicate efforts by developing an entire ERP when its role is already addressed in the local contingency plan. The hospital should consult with the Joint Commission on Accreditation of Healthcare Organizations (JCAHO, the Joint Commission) in determining the complete requirements for its ERP.

Ideally, employers within the community will have coordinated emergency response planning with the hospital prior to any emergency event. However, the hospital may need to treat contaminated victims of emergency incidents without the benefit of pre-emergency planning. Both scenarios need to be addressed in the hospital's ERP.

When required, an ERP must be prepared even if community coordination has not been initiated or completed. The hospital's ERP must be in writing and established prior to an actual emergency. All employees and affiliated personnel expected to be involved in an emergency response, including physicians and nurses as well as maintenance employees and other ancillary staff, should be familiar with the details of the plan.

Elements of a Hospital Emergency Response Plan

The hospital's ERP should address the following elements:

- Pre-emergency drills implementing the ERP;
- Practice sessions with other local emergency response organizations using the ICS;
- Personnel roles and responsibilities, including who will be in charge of directing the response, training, and communications;
- Lines of authority and communication between the incident site and hospital personnel regarding hazards and potential contamination;
- Designation of a decontamination team, including emergency department physicians, nurses, aides, and support personnel;
- Description of the hospital's system for immediately accessing information on toxic materials;
- Evacuation plan and designation of alternative facilities that could provide treatment in case of contamination of the hospital's Emergency Department;
- Plan for managing emergency treatment of non-contaminated patients;
- Decontamination equipment, procedures, and designation of decontamination areas (either indoors or outdoors);
- Hospital staff use of PPE based on hazards present or likely to be present, routes of exposure, degree of contact, and each individual's specific tasks;
- Location and quantity of PPE;
- Prevention of cross-contamination by airborne substances via the hospital's ventilation system or other means;
- Prevention of cross-contamination by hazardous substances that are not airborne (e.g., surface contamination);
- Air monitoring to ensure that the facility is safe for occupancy following treatment of contaminated patients; and
- Post-emergency critique and follow-up of drills and actual emergencies.

Preplanning

A hospital designated as a decontamination facility must prepare to fulfill its role in community emergency response. This is accomplished by engaging in emergency response planning activities that involve all segments of the community (i.e., employers, other emergency response organizations, local government and the emergency medical community). Pre-planning with the LEPC should include the identification, inventory, and location of known chemical hazards in the community; this includes information gathered from Material Safety Data Sheets (MSDSs). With this in mind, the hospital should consider the following:

- The hospital must define its role in community emergency response by pre-planning and coordinating with other local emergency response organizations, such as the fire department. In particular, the hospital must be familiar with the ICS used by other local organizations during emergencies and should participate in training and practice sessions using the ICS.

- Training must be based on the duties and responsibilities of each employee.

- Hospitals should have a contingency plan for managing other patients in the emergency response system when contaminated patients are being treated.

- There should be communication between other members of the ICS, the incident site, and the hospital personnel regarding the hazards associated with potential contaminants.

- Hospitals should have access to a database that is compiled by the LEPC to provide immediate information to hospital staff on the hazards associated with exposure to toxic materials that may be used by local employers.

Training Employees

HAZWOPER requires varying levels of training for personnel responding to emergencies involving hazardous substances or

cleanup. HAZWOPER is a performance-based regulation allowing individual employers flexibility in meeting the requirements of the regulation in the most cost-effective manner. It is not OSHA's intent that every member of a community's emergency response services receive high levels of specialized hazardous materials training. The community may determine that it is appropriate for the fire department to develop a small group of highly trained hazardous materials technicians and specialists, called a "HAZMAT team," or may find that the community does not require a HAZMAT team and that less intensive training is adequate.

To determine the appropriate level and type of training under HAZWOPER, hospitals need to consider the hazards in their community and determine what capabilities will be required to respond effectively to those hazards. This determination is to be based on reasonably anticipated worst-case scenarios. All individuals must be adequately trained to perform their anticipated job duties without endangering themselves or others.

Emergency medical service (EMS) personnel (e.g., emergency medical technicians [EMTs] and ambulance corps members) are often the first on the scene and, therefore, are likely to witness or discover a release of a hazardous substance. As a result, they generally need First Responder Awareness Level[2] training as a minimum. (Refer to 29 CFR 1910.120(q)(6)(i).) There is no minimum number of training hours required, but the training must be sufficient or the employees must have had sufficient experience to demonstrate specific competencies. EMS personnel who have received only Awareness Level training must not be involved in the transport or treatment of contaminated patients. EMS personnel who transport or treat contaminated patients at the release area must be trained to the First Responder Operations Level.[3]

Medical personnel who will decontaminate victims must be trained to the First Responder Operations Level with emphasis on

[2]Awareness Level training enables employees to recognize an emergency event and notify the appropriate authorities.

[3]Operations Level training enables employees to respond initially to a hazardous substance release and to take defensive action to protect people, property and the environment.

the use of PPE and decontamination procedures. (Refer to 29 CFR 1910.120(q)(6)(ii).) Individuals who develop the decontamination procedures and select PPE for the employees who assist in the decontamination of patients must also be trained to the First Responder Operations Level with additional training in decontamination procedures. The employer must certify that personnel are trained to safely perform their job duties and responsibilities. This includes a minimum of 8 hours of training or demonstrated competencies and an annual refresher. Hospitals may develop an in-house training course on decontamination, PPE use, and other measures to prevent the spread of contamination to other portions of the hospital. Alternatively, hospitals may provide additional site-specific training in decontamination and PPE use after sending personnel to a First Responder Operations Level course.

Every member of the emergency room clinical staff who is expected to treat contaminated victims, plus any employee who might be exposed to hazardous substances during an emergency response incident, should be (1) familiar with how the hospital intends to respond to hazardous substance incidents, (2) trained in the appropriate use of PPE, and (3) required to participate in scheduled drills. Such a pre-designated decontamination team might consist of emergency physicians, emergency department nurses and aides, and other support personnel, such as respiratory therapists, security, and maintenance personnel.

In emergency situations, other hospital personnel who are not expected to decontaminate patents may need to enter the decontamination area to perform necessary functions. These employees may be considered Skilled Support Personnel (e.g., medical specialist or a trade person, such as an electrician). Skilled Support Personnel must be given an initial briefing, at the time of the incident, including instruction in the wearing of appropriate PPE, what hazards are involved, and what duties are to be performed.

All hospital employees, including ancillary personnel, such as housekeeping and laundry staff, must be adequately trained to perform their assigned job duties in a safe and healthful manner. If ancillary personnel will be expected to clean up the decontamination area, they must be trained in accordance with 29 CFR 1910.120(q)(11) and have access to MSDSs for those chemicals

that may be used to decontaminate equipment and the area. Coordination with community resources for cleanup assistance must be included in the contingency plan.

Documenting Training

Employees need not necessarily receive a certificate, but the employer must certify training with some form of documentation (Note: The HAZWOPER standard does not contain a specific certification requirement for Awareness Level training, but employees must be able to demonstrate the required competencies). It is considered good practice to provide employees with a training certificate as well as to document the training in the employer's records. The hospital also must document, in its ERP, its training plan for personnel who respond to hazardous substance incidents and to contaminated victims.

Performing Emergency Drills

Drills are required under SARA, Title III, as part of the local contingency plan and should also be performed as part of pre-emergency planning under HAZWOPER. Emergency medical responders should be involved in drills through the LEPC. Where facilities may be using/relying on mutual aid, those parties should also participate in drills.

The Joint Commission requires accredited hospitals to perform emergency drills in accordance with their emergency response plan twice a year. This may be fulfilled from a planned drill or responding to an actual emergency.

Responding to Emergencies

Once an emergency actually occurs, the benefits of pre-planning will be immediately apparent, especially in identifying the hazardous substance(s) involved. First Responder Awareness Level

and Hazard Communication training enables responders to determine the likely presence or release of a hazardous substance. Data from those at the scene of the incident may identify or help identify hazards. Resources, including printed reference materials, computer databases, and telephone hotlines, are available to help identify hazards not immediately recognized. The U.S. Department of Transportation (DOT) requires that a 24-hour-a-day telephone number be available from the chemical producer or shipper to assist the emergency response community in getting accurate information on chemical hazards.

Selecting PPE

Hospitals must evaluate the potential hazardous exposures of their employees and provide appropriate PPE. PPE selection must be based on a hazard assessment that identifies the hazards that employees might reasonably be anticipated to encounter under worst-case scenarios. Consideration must also be given to those emergency medical personnel who would be exposed to hazardous substances because they are expected to treat contaminated patients at the hazardous substance release area (i.e., EMS personnel).

Potential exposures of hospital staff and EMS personnel usually result from proximity to or contact with a patient whose skin and/or clothing may be contaminated with hazardous substances. Anticipated exposures are likely to include airborne or absorption hazards from a patient whose skin or clothing has come in contact with hazardous liquids or has been contaminated with hazardous particles. The hospital staff must be provided with PPE sufficient for the type of hazard and exposure levels an employee can reasonably anticipate from such incidents, and planning must consider the hospital's role under community emergency response plans.

Other medical personnel (e.g., ambulance drivers) whose expected job duties do not include treating contaminated

patients may be needed to respond to accidents where hazards may be present. These employees must be provided with and receive instruction in the wearing of appropriate PPE, any limitations of the PPE, the hazards involved, and all other appropriate safety and health precautions which may include respiratory protection and hazard communication.

Personnel who will be involved in decontamination must be equipped with PPE that is appropriate for the hazardous substances expected to be encountered. Sources of helpful information include:

- OSHA Publication 3249: "Best Practices for Hospital-Based First Receivers of Victims from Mass Casualty Incidents Involving the Release of Hazardous Substances" ("First Receivers" document).

- Reference guidebooks, database networks, MSDSs, and telephone hotlines may also be useful in determining suitable PPE.

- Communication with those at the scene of the incident (this will be helpful in identifying the type of PPE that will be required to prevent secondary contamination of the hospital personnel).

Factors to be considered in the selection of PPE include toxicity, routes of exposure, degree of contact, and the specific task assigned to the user. The primary routes of exposure are inhalation, ingestion, and direct contact.

Types of PPE range from gloves to chemical protective clothing to respiratory protection. The proper use of PPE requires considerable training by a competent person, such as a health and safety professional, and is required under OSHA's standard on Personal Protective Equipment, 29 CFR 1910.132. Wearing PPE without proper training can pose significant hazards to the wearer.

Selecting Respirators

To determine which respirator is needed, hospitals can consult OSHA's Respiratory Protection standard, 29 CFR 1910.134. The standard includes requirements for respirator selection, medical evaluation, fit testing, respirator use, inspecting and cleaning, training, and program evaluation. Employees must not be assigned to tasks requiring the use of respirators unless it has been determined that they are physically able to perform the work and use the respirator. This medical determination must be made by a physician or other licensed health care professional. OSHA offers a respiratory protection eTool at www.osha.gov to assist employers in complying with the standard.

The selection of respirators necessary to protect employees when they are decontaminating patients, responding to emergency incidents, or otherwise being exposed to hazardous substances depends on a number of factors (e.g., type of contaminant, physical state, volatility, and toxicity). As discussed previously for general PPE, the employer must perform a hazard assessment to characterize potential employee exposures and select appropriate respirators for those employees based on reasonably anticipated hazards. The "First Receivers" document provides more specific information regarding respiratory protection appropriate for first receivers based on a hospital's status and potential exposure conditions.

Decontaminating Patients

Ideally, when medically appropriate, patients should be decontaminated before reaching the hospital, preferably at the incident site. However, complete on-site decontamination of victims may not be possible due to the medical conditions of the victims as well as other factors, such as emergency responder training and skill levels, weather conditions, and equipment availability.

Therefore, the hospital should have designated decontamination areas.

Although areas dedicated solely to decontamination need not be set aside, hospitals need to take appropriate precautions to prevent the spread of contamination to other areas within the hospital. Decontamination should be performed in areas of the facility that will minimize any exposures to uncontaminated employees, other patients, visitors, or equipment. Morgues are often used as decontamination rooms because of their preexisting drainage and ventilation systems. Morgues often have ventilation isolation to prevent mixing of airflow with other area systems.

An alternative to an indoor decontamination area would be an outside or portable decontamination facility. This might include wading pools or outdoor showers, along with bags for disposal of contaminated clothes. Contaminated drainage resulting from the decontamination process must be disposed of in accordance with federal, state, and local regulations.

Preparing to Receive Victims

Once word reaches the hospital of a hazardous substance incident, all hospital personnel engaged in the response should be notified of the nature of the emergency and the type of contamination expected. Then, the hospital should outfit all necessary personnel with appropriate PPE.

All persons along the route from the emergency entrance to the decontamination area need to be relocated. This area may need to be protected by plastic or paper sheeting and the area outside the emergency department entrance set up to direct the flow of contaminated patients to the decontamination area.

Avoiding Cross-Contamination

Airborne contaminants may be transported via the hospital's ventilation system. Therefore, ventilation in the decontamination area should be separate from that for the rest of the hospital. As mentioned earlier, morgues with an isolated ventilation system are often used as decontamination rooms.

If a contaminated victim is emitting unknown or highly toxic airborne contaminants or if the ventilation system recirculates air to other parts of the hospital, the ventilation system in the decontamination area should be turned off. However, where chemicals are involved, not all of them will be volatile enough to cause off-gassing. Because Emergency Department personnel could be at risk if the ventilation system is shut off during decontamination in an enclosed area, ambient air should be monitored, and the plan should provide means of supplementary or auxiliary ventilation. Prior to restarting the ventilation system, air monitoring is advised to assure that the atmosphere is safe for circulation. The use of direct-reading instruments to evaluate air quality must be done by an individual who has been properly trained in the use of the instruments.

In addition to concerns relating to airborne contaminants and facility ventilation systems, consideration must be given to potential surface contamination of equipment, work surfaces, and other areas. For example, an ambulance stretcher used for transport of a contaminated patient needs to be properly decontaminated to prevent the spread of contamination to other areas, patients, or hospital personnel. The hospital's ERP should include provisions for decontaminating surface contaminants and for the containment and disposal of equipment and materials that cannot be safely decontaminated.

To learn more about HAZWOPER or other OSHA standards, contact your regional OSHA office listed at the end of this publication.

Related Standards

For further information on applicable standards, refer to:

- 29 CFR 1910.38 (Emergency Action Plans),
- 29 CFR 1910.39 (Fire Prevention Plans),
- 29 CFR 1910.120/1926.65 (Hazardous Waste Operations and Emergency Response),
- 29 CFR 1910.132 (Personal Protective Equipment),
- 29 CFR 1910.134 (Respiratory Protection),
- 29 CFR 1910.1030 (Bloodborne Pathogens), and
- 29 CFR 1910.1200 (Hazard Communication [Appendix A - Health Hazard Definitions; Appendix B - Hazard Determination; Appendix C - Information Sources]).

Additional Resources

Emergency Planning and Community Right-to-Know Act (EPCRA) Hotline, Phone: 1-800-424-9346, Fax: (703) 412-3333, www.epa.gov.

Joint Commission on Accreditation of Healthcare Organizations, (JCAHO) Phone: 630-792-5000, www.jointcommission.org.

United States Department of Health and Human Services. Agency for Healthcare Research and Quality (AHRQ). "Preparedness for Chemical, Biological, Radiological, Nuclear, and Explosive Events; Questionnaire for Health Care Facilities." www.ahrq.gov.

References

1. OSHA Publication 3249, "Best Practices for Hospital-Based First Receivers of Victims from Mass Casualty Incidents Involving the Release of Hazardous Substances" ("First Receivers" document) (August 2005).

2. Joint Commission on Accreditation of Healthcare Organizations. "Management of the Environment of Care" chapter. 2006 Comprehensive Accreditation Manual for Hospitals: The Official Handbook (CAMH). Oakbrook Terrace, Illinois (2006).

3. U.S. Department of Health and Human Services. Public Health Service, Agency for Toxic Substances and Disease Registry, Volume I, (revised). Emergency Medical Services: A Planning Guide for the Management of Contaminated Patients. Atlanta, Georgia (2000).

4. U.S. Department of Health and Human Services. Public Health Service, Agency for Toxic Substances and Disease Registry. Managing Hazardous Materials Incidents, Volume II, (revised). Hospital Emergency Departments: A Planning Guide for the Management of Contaminated Patients. Atlanta, Georgia (2000).

5. Public Law No. 99-499, "The Superfund Amendments and Reauthorization Act of 1986," Title III.

6. State of California Emergency Medical Services Authority. Hazardous Materials Medical Management Protocols. Sacramento, California, second edition (1991).

7. "CDC Recommendations for Civilian Communities Near Chemical Weapons Depots: Guidelines for Medical Preparedness," 60 *Federal Register* (123): 3308 (June 27, 1995).

OSHA Assistance

OSHA can provide extensive help through a variety of programs, including technical assistance about effective safety and health programs, state plans, workplace consultations, voluntary protection programs, strategic partnerships, training and education, and more. An overall commitment to workplace safety and health can add value to your business, to your workplace, and to your life.

Safety and Health Program Management Guidelines

Effective management of employee safety and health protection is a decisive factor in reducing the extent and severity of work-related injuries and illnesses and their related costs. In fact, an effective safety and health program forms the basis of good employee protection and can save time and money (about $4 for every dollar spent) and increase productivity and reduce employee injuries, illnesses, and related workers' compensation costs.

To assist employers and employees in developing effective safety and health programs, OSHA published recommended Safety and Health Program Management Guidelines (54 *Federal Register* (16): 3904-3916, January 26, 1989). These voluntary guidelines can be applied to all places of employment covered by OSHA.

The guidelines identify four general elements critical to the development of a successful safety and health management system:

- Management leadership and employee involvement,
- Worksite analysis,
- Hazard prevention and control, and
- Safety and health training.

The guidelines recommend specific actions, under each of those general elements, to achieve an effective safety and health program. The Federal Register notice is available online at www.osha.gov.

State Programs

The Occupational Safety and Health Act of 1970 (OSH Act) encourages states to develop and operate their own job safety and health plans. OSHA approves and monitors these plans. Twenty-

four states, Puerto Rico, and the Virgin Islands currently operate approved state plans: 22 cover both private and public (state and local government) employment; Connecticut, New Jersey, New York, and the Virgin Islands cover the public sector only. States and territories with their own OSHA-approved occupational safety and health plans must adopt standards identical to, or at least as effective as, the Federal OSHA standards.

Consultation Services

Consultation assistance is available on request to employers who want help in establishing and maintaining a safe and healthful workplace. Largely funded by OSHA, the service is provided at no cost to the employer. Primarily developed for smaller employers with more hazardous operations, the consultation service is delivered by state governments employing professional safety and health consultants. Comprehensive assistance includes an appraisal of all mechanical systems, work practices, and occupational safety and health hazards of the workplace and all aspects of the employer's present job safety and health program. In addition, the service offers assistance to employers in developing and implementing an effective safety and health program. No penalties are proposed or citations issued for hazards identified by the consultant. OSHA provides consultation assistance to the employer with the assurance that his or her name and firm and any information about the workplace will not be routinely reported to OSHA enforcement staff.

Under the consultation program, certain exemplary employers may request participation in OSHA's Safety and Health Achievement Recognition Program (SHARP). Eligibility for participation in SHARP includes receiving a comprehensive consultation visit, demonstrating exemplary achievements in workplace safety and health by abating all identified hazards, and developing an excellent safety and health program.

Employers accepted into SHARP may receive an exemption from programmed inspections (not complaint or accident investigation inspections) for a period of 1 year. For more information concerning consultation assistance, see OSHA's website at www.osha.gov.

Voluntary Protection Programs (VPP)

Voluntary Protection Programs and on-site consultation services, when coupled with an effective enforcement program, expand employee protection to help meet the goals of the OSH Act. The VPPs motivate others to achieve excellent safety and health results in the same outstanding way as they establish a cooperative relationship between employers, employees, and OSHA.

For additional information on VPP and how to apply, contact the OSHA regional offices listed at the end of this publication.

Strategic Partnership Program

OSHA's Strategic Partnership Program, the newest member of OSHA's cooperative programs, helps encourage, assist, and recognize the efforts of partners to eliminate serious workplace hazards and achieve a high level of employee safety and health. Whereas OSHA's Consultation Program and VPP entail one-on-one relationships between OSHA and individual worksites, most strategic partnerships seek to have a broader impact by building cooperative relationships with groups of employers and employees. These partnerships are voluntary, cooperative relationships between OSHA, employers, employee representatives, and others (e.g., trade unions, trade and professional associations, universities, and other government agencies).

For more information on this and other cooperative programs, contact your nearest OSHA office, or visit OSHA's website at www.osha.gov.

Alliance Program

Through the Alliance Program, OSHA works with groups committed to safety and health, including businesses, trade or professional organizations, unions and educational institutions, to leverage resources and expertise to develop compliance assistance tools and resources and share information with employers and employees to help prevent injuries, illnesses and fatalities in the workplace.

Alliance program agreements have been established with a wide variety of industries including meat, apparel, poultry, steel, plastics, maritime, printing, chemical, construction, paper and telecommuni-

cations. These agreements are addressing many safety and health hazards and at-risk audiences, including silica, fall protection, amputations, immigrant workers, youth and small businesses. By meeting the goals of the Alliance Program agreements (training and education, outreach and communication, and promoting the national dialogue on workplace safety and health), OSHA and the Alliance Program participants are developing and disseminating compliance assistance information and resources for employers and employees such as electronic assistance tools, fact sheets, toolbox talks, and training programs.

OSHA Training and Education

OSHA area offices offer a variety of information services, such as compliance assistance, technical advice, publications, audiovisual aids, and speakers for special engagements. OSHA's Training Institute in Arlington Heights, IL, provides basic and advanced courses in safety and health for Federal and state compliance officers, state consultants, Federal agency personnel, and private sector employers, employees, and their representatives.

The OSHA Training Institute also has established OSHA Training Institute Education Centers to address the increased demand for its courses from the private sector and from other federal agencies. These centers include colleges, universities, and nonprofit training organizations that have been selected after a competition for participation in the program.

OSHA also provides funds to nonprofit organizations, through grants, to conduct workplace training and education in subjects where OSHA believes there is a lack of workplace training. Grants are awarded annually. Grant recipients are expected to contribute 20 percent of the total grant cost.

For more information on training and education, contact the OSHA Training Institute, Directorate of Training and Education, 2020 South Arlington Heights Road, Arlington Heights, IL, 60005, (847) 297-4810, or see Training on OSHA's website at www.osha.gov. For further information on any OSHA program, contact your nearest OSHA regional office listed at the end of this publication.

Information Available Electronically

OSHA has a variety of materials and tools available on its website at www.osha.gov. These include electronic compliance assistance tools, such as *Safety and Health Topics Pages, eTools, Expert Advisors;* regulations, directives, publications and videos; and other information for employers and employees. OSHA's software programs and compliance assistance tools walk you through challenging safety and health issues and common problems to find the best solutions for your workplace.

A wide variety of OSHA materials, including standards, interpretations, directives, and more can be purchased on CD-ROM from the U.S. Government Printing Office, Superintendent of Documents, toll-free phone (866) 512-1800.

OSHA Publications

OSHA has an extensive publications program. For a listing of free or sales items, visit OSHA's website at www.osha.gov or contact the OSHA Publications Office, U.S. Department of Labor, 200 Constitution Avenue, NW, N-3101, Washington, DC 20210: Telephone (202) 693-1888 or fax to (202) 693-2498.

Contacting OSHA

To report an emergency, file a complaint, or seek OSHA advice, assistance, or products, call (800) 321-OSHA or contact your nearest OSHA Regional office listed at the end of this publication. The teletypewriter (TTY) number is (877) 889-5627.

Written correspondence can be mailed to the nearest OSHA Regional or Area Office listed at the end of this publication or to OSHA's national office at: U.S. Department of Labor, Occupational Safety and Health Administration, 200 Constitution Avenue, N.W., Washington, DC 20210.

By visiting OSHA's website at www.osha.gov, you can also:

- File a complaint online,
- Submit general inquiries about workplace safety and health electronically, and
- Find more information about OSHA and occupational safety and health.

www.osha.gov

OSHA Regional Offices

Region I
(CT,* ME, MA, NH, RI, VT*)
JFK Federal Building, Room E340
Boston, MA 02203
(617) 565-9860

Region II
(NJ,* NY,* PR,* VI*)
201 Varick Street, Room 670
New York, NY 10014
(212) 337-2378

Region III
(DE, DC, MD,* PA, VA,* WV)
The Curtis Center
170 S. Independence Mall West
Suite 740 West
Philadelphia, PA 19106-3309
(215) 861-4900

Region IV
(AL, FL, GA, KY,* MS, NC,* SC,* TN*)
61 Forsyth Street, SW, Room 6T50
Atlanta, GA 30303
(404) 562-2300

Region V
(IL, IN,* MI,* MN,* OH, WI)
230 South Dearborn Street
Room 3244
Chicago, IL 60604
(312) 353-2220

Region VI
(AR, LA, NM,* OK, TX)
525 Griffin Street, Room 602
Dallas, TX 75202
(972) 850-4145

Region VII
(IA,* KS, MO, NE)
Two Pershing Square
2300 Main Street, Suite 1010
Kansas City, MO 64108-2416
(816) 283-8745

Region VIII
(CO, MT, NO, SO, UT,* WY*)
1999 Broadway, Suite 1690
PO Box 46550
Denver, CO 80202-5716
(720) 264-6550

Region IX
(American Samoa, AZ,* CA,* HI,*
NV,* GM,
Northern Mariana Islands)
90 7th Street, Suite 18-100
San Francisco, CA 94103
(415) 625-2547

Region X
(AK,* ID, OR,* WA*)
1111 Third Avenue, Suite 715
Seattle, WA 98101-3212
(206) 553-5930

   * These states and territories operate their own OSHA-approved job safety and health programs and cover state and local government employees as well as private sector employees. The Connecticut, New Jersey, New York and Virgin Islands plans cover public employees only. States with approved programs must have standards that are identical to, or at least as effective as, the Federal standards.

   Note: To get contact information for OSHA Area Offices, OSHA-approved State Plans and OSHA Consultation Projects, please visit us online at www.osha.gov or call us at 1-800-321-OSHA.

www.ingramcontent.com/pod-product-compliance
Lightning Source LLC
Chambersburg PA
CBHW071601170526
45166CB00004B/1751